ZOOS

Miriam Moss

The Bookwright Press
New York · 1987

Topics

The Age of Dinosaurs
Airports
Ancient Peoples
Archaeology
Bridges
Castles
Costumes and Clothes
Earthquakes and Volcanoes
Energy
Fairs and Circuses
Farm Animals
Ghosts and the Supernatural
Great Disasters
Helicopters
Houses and Homes

Inventions
Jungles
Maps and Globes
Money
Musical Instruments
People of the World
Photography
Pollution and Conservation
Prisons and Punishment
Robots
Spacecraft
Television
Trees of the World
Under the Ground
Zoos

First published in the
United States in 1987 by
The Bookwright Press
387 Park Avenue South
New York, NY 10016

First published in 1987 by
Wayland (Publishers) Limited
61 Western Road, Hove
East Sussex BN3 1JD, England

© Copyright 1987 Wayland (Publishers) Ltd

ISBN 0–531–18148–0
Library of Congress Catalog Card Number: 86–73116

Phototypeset by
Kalligrahics Ltd, Redhill, Surrey
Printed in Belgium by
Casterman sa, Tournai

All the words that appear
in **bold** are explained in the
glossary on page 30.

Contents

The First Zoos

Humans have kept animals for thousands of years. The earliest known collection of animals was in Iraq in the Middle East in the third century B.C. The ancient Egyptians, Chinese and Romans kept **menageries** with which they entertained crowds. These animals were often treated with extreme cruelty.

This tomb painting shows the types of animals kept in menageries in ancient Egypt.

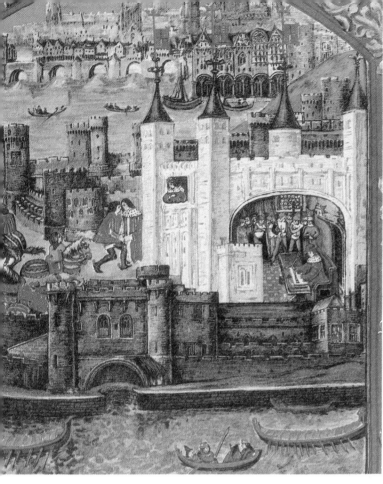

The Tower of London, where Henry III kept his collection of animals.

In the thirteenth century Henry III of England kept lions, **lynxes**, leopards, camels and a polar bear in the Tower of London. The polar bear was taken down the Thames River every evening to fish for its supper. Later, in the eighteenth century, the public was allowed into the Tower to see the menagerie for the first time. They either paid a penny or they brought a cat or a dog

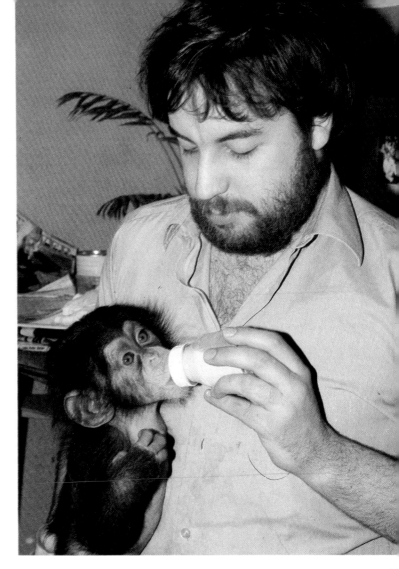

A keeper at the London Zoo. One of his many jobs is to feed a young chimpanzee who could not be fed by its mother.

with them to be fed to the lions!

Finally all the animals were given to the Zoological Society of London, which was founded in 1826. This was to become the London Zoo. The zoo was first opened to the public in 1847. It still has one of the largest collections of animals in the world.

Today, zoos need to attract as many people as possible to come and see the animals. Their entrance fees are needed to keep zoos open and well equipped. Without the public's help, zoos would not be able to survive. Most good modern zoos want people to enjoy looking at the animals, but they are not there just for entertainment. Zoos also want people to learn about the animals. Many zoos have a special area where adults and children can see, touch and study the animals. At the Arizona-

Besides providing shelter and safety for the animals, zoos are centers for adults and children to learn about the animals of the world.

Sonoran Desert Museum in the Southwest, visitors can actually handle **tarantulas** and rattlesnakes. This helps them to overcome their fear of poisonous animals.

Zoos also offer important information by providing talks, walks, films and magazines. Zoos want people to help save wild animals that are in danger of becoming **extinct**. Today's zoo acts as an "ark," rather like Noah's Ark

For these two tiger cats, the Arizon-Sonoran Desert Museum, is a safe "ark."

This zebra has been put to sleep for a short time, so that the zoo vet can examine it. Vets can greatly help the zoo scientists in their study of the animals.

in the Bible story – a safe place where animals can breed and increase in numbers.

Having rare animals in zoos means that the zoo scientists can study them very closely. The scientists need to learn as much as they can about the animals if they are to help save their **species** from extinction.

Taking Care of the Animals

The people who take care of the animals each day are called zoo keepers. The keepers start work early in the morning. They change into their overalls and rubber boots, pick up a stiff broom, a bucket, a hose pipe, some **disinfectant** and a shovel and go to the animal **enclosures** to clean them out. Then they prepare the animals'

Part of a zoo keeper's busy day is to clean out the animal enclosures. In this case, the elephant needs to be cleaned as well!

meals for the day in freshly scrubbed steel dishes. The keepers give a list of all the food they might need for the week to the senior keeper who orders it from the zoo's food store.

It is important that the animals are given the right kind of **diet**. Some animals need special foods to keep them healthy. For example, a vampire bat needs one cup of fresh blood a day and the apes like blackcurrant juice. The reindeer need a **lichen** that is imported from Iceland and the flamingos need to eat a

Penguins are fed by hand, by their keeper, since they will not pick the fish up from the ground. Each type of animal is given a carefully planned diet to suit its needs.

An Asiatic elephant reaches out to the crowds. This enclosure is not good for the elephant, since the public can feed it from where they are standing.

special dye that keeps their feathers brightly colored. The ant-eater, instead of eating ants as you would expect, prefers canned meat, milk and raw eggs.

While the keepers feed their animals they keep a watchful eye on their behavior and see that each animal is getting enough to eat. In the afternoon the keepers may spend some time with the public, answering questions as well as being on the look out for people who might be frightening the animals.

The keepers have to watch the animals too, as some people feed them, which is unnecessary. It can also be dangerous as it can make animals very ill. At the end of each day, the keepers make sure that the animals are fed and comfortable for the night before they fill in their daily reports.

If any animal appears to be sick, the keeper will call the vet immediately. Perhaps an eagle has a fractured leg, a puff adder has a

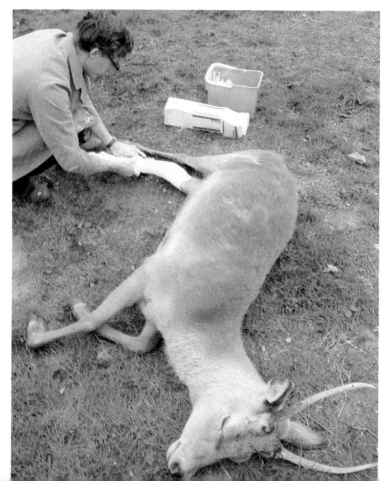

A young red deer stag receives treatment for a broken leg from the vet. The stag feels no pain because he has been given an injection to make him go to sleep.

13

swollen face, or a crocodile is suffering from a toothache!

The vet's job is not only to treat sick animals. He or she also gives regular health checkups, trims hooves, **vaccinates** against disease, **worms** animals and takes care of new arrivals in **quarantine**. Vets, along with the zoo scientists, also study the animals. Any new information that might help other zoos is passed all around the world.

Zoos also breed rare animals that are not able to reproduce in their natural surroundings, and then they release them into the wild.

In the San Diego Wild Animal Park, visitors can view the animals from overhead walkways. The animals have plenty of space without the dangers of their natural habitats.

The black rhino is threatened by extinction. These rhinos, however, are only safe in this Kenyan game reserve because they are protected by the game wardens.

The San Diego Wild Animal Park in Caifornia is linked to the famous San Diego Zoo. Both are enormous, having over 1,000 species. The wild animal park has huge enclosures where scientists can study and breed many different kinds of rare animals.

Endangered species are still being taken from the wild by people who sell them for money. The shy, plant-eating mountain gorilla of Central Africa is captured by **poachers,** and humans destroy huge areas of its forest **habitat** every day. Since 1980, the number of black rhino in Africa has fallen from 15,000 to 5,000. Poachers kill

Within the protective surroundings of a zoo, this scimitar-horned oryx was able to breed and give birth to her offspring.

the rhino for their horns, which are then carved or ground down to make medicines for people in eastern Asia.

Scientists and **conservationists** are working hard to save these animals from extinction. Recently three zoos in Britain bred enough scimitar-horned **oryx** to send the first five pairs back to a national park in Tunisia, North Africa, where they had been extinct for more than forty years.

Animal Homes

Good modern zoos make sure that their animal homes (enclosures) meet first, the needs of the animals; second, the needs of the keepers; and third, the needs of the public.

People who design the enclosures need to know about the animals' original homes in the wild. A good enclosure should give the animal the right kind of space and be as similar as possible to the animal's natural habitat. The Topeka Zoo,

The Cologne Zoo in West Germany has taken great care to make this humming bird's home as similar as possible to its natural, tropical surroundings.

in Kansas, has a special building that contains a tropical **rain forest**. La Fortune North American Living Museum, which is part of the Tulsa Zoo in Oklahoma, has four buildings, each one with a different climate. Frankfurt Zoo in West Germany is equipped with a special crocodile jungle.

Other zoos have **expedition** trails, like the Port Lymne Wildlife Sanctuary in Britain, or the Metro Toronto Zoo in Canada, which takes

A short-nosed crocodile in an African zoo. It is hard to believe that it is not in its natural surroundings.

An African gazelle and her young offspring are kept together in the Frankfurt Zoo, West Germany, safe from other animals and the dangers of the wild.

visitors through wooded valleys on a quiet electric train to see the grizzly bears and the wood **bison**. Another Canadian trail involves skiing across country to watch the Siberian tigers rolling in the snow.

For the animals to be content, they need to be specially grouped. Male animals are kept apart from the female and her young if they are not found together in the wild. The animals' homes should provide shelter, warmth and a quiet place for the female to have her young. Shy animals like antelopes need

The rhinoceros iguanas' natural habitat is the desert, so they are used to living under the great heat of the sun. Because of this, they need extra warmth from heat lamps in their zoo enclosures.

quiet areas too, away from the noise of the public; whereas otters need plenty of water to swim in and a dry sleeping box.

The enclosures should be at the right temperature for each particular species and should have suitable lighting. Some **reptiles** need heated floors and warm spotlights. In some modern zoos, **nocturnal animals** like bats and bush babies live in "reversed" light conditions so they will be active during the daytime. During the day they are given light that is like moonlight to play in. In the evening, when the zoo closes, the lights are turned up as bright as daylight. Then the animals go to sleep as they would during the day in the wild.

Good enclosures should have safe barriers to keep the visitors and the animals apart. Sometimes a ditch full of water is enough for animals that dislike water. At other times a low fence or bank is enough for small animals that cannot climb.

All the creatures in a zoo have different types of enclosures to suit their needs. This blond porpoise has a huge pool to swim in.

In the polar bear enclosure at Munich Zoo in West Germany, the barrier is a pane of glass. You can watch the bears glide by underwater, in their huge glass tank, just a few inches from your nose. At the Miami Monkey Jungle Zoo in the Florida, most of the public walkways are enclosed with wire netting so that the monkeys can move around freely. It is the humans that are enclosed!

Bad enclosures lead to sad, unnatural behavior in zoo animals. You can easily see when

Although this beach looks real, it has been specially built for the wading birds at Vogelpark, Walsrode in West Germany. It even has a machine that make waves.

an animal is unhappy. Big cats and bears in cramped enclosures have a habit of endlessly pacing up and down the length of the cage. Bored parrots groom themselves and each other too much and get bald patches. Animals need to be kept occupied.

At the Panaewa Rainforest Zoo in Hawaii there are computerized

Behind the bars of a small cage is not the right place for this beautiful tiger. Poorly planned, inadequate enclosures leave the animals unhappy and bored.

Keeping the animals entertained is a very important part of their happiness. This panda in the Beijing Zoo, China, is enjoying a game with its keeper on the climbing frame.

games for the tigers to keep them from getting bored. They chase and "kill" a mechanical squirrel, and visitors can set off electric noises that encourage the tigers to jump and stalk. In the Brookfield Zoo in Chicago, the sand cats from Asia live in a desertlike enclosure that is stocked with live insects for them to hunt.

A Safe Ark

Zoos today have come a long way since the early eighteenth century when it was believed that gorillas should be fed on the "best" diet available, which was thought to be black grapes, steak and port wine.

People are now much more wary of taking animals from the wild without caring about the future of the species. The zoos of the world come in many shapes and sizes.

In Australia, young koalas are cared for and bottle-fed by their zoo keepers.

Some still house their animals in poor, cramped conditions although with better laws about how animals should be kept, these zoos are slowly disappearing.

Another kind of zoo is a **safari park**. At Windsor Safari Park in England, the animals are fenced inside huge areas of land. Visitors drive through the park looking at the animals from their vehicles.

Many zoos specialize in keeping local, or native animals. Tama Zoological Park in Japan has a special insect house that

Some visitors to a wildlife park being viewed at close quarters by a Wapiti stag.

This experiment to see if the baby of a rare species (the bongo) could be born from the body of another, more common animal (the eland) was successful. It is necessary to carry out this type of experiment with endangered species, so that a greater number can be bred.

contains a spectacular butterfly farm and a firefly farm. At the Bergen Aquarium in Norway, visitors watch a superb collection of northern sea creatures from underwater viewing rooms.

Other zoos are famous for their breeding successes. Burgers Zoo and Safari Park in the Netherlands has a large chimpanzee colony and Twycross Zoo in England specializes in breeding apes and monkeys. The Hawaiian goose, the Galapagos giant turtle, Przewalski's horse and the Barbary lion are just some of the animals that were in serious danger of extinction in the wild but have been saved by being bred in large enough numbers in a zoo – a safe "ark."

Zoos have always been, and still are, criticized for denying animals their freedom. The animal **liberation** groups of the world believe that all animals should live in their natural habitats and not in enclosures, but they realize that it is sometimes necessary to take animals from the wild for their own

These very rare golden monkeys are content with their enclosure. They are grooming and cleaning each other as they would in the wild.

safety. It is also realized that even though zoos are very unnatural places for wild animals to live, without them many species would have become extinct or would certainly be in grave danger of extinction now.

Zoos are not just for the entertainment of the public, but places where animals can breed and live in safety; where research can be done to help prevent further extinction and where people can learn more about the animals of the world and learn to care for them.

Without the care and attention offered at the Bristol Zoo in England, this white tiger cub would probably not have been born, and its species would have been even closer to extinction.

Glossary

Bison A wild ox.

Conservationist A person who believes in protecting natural resources, including animals.

Diet A planned selection of food.

Disinfectant A chemical that destroys germs.

Enclosure A fenced or walled area.

Expedition An organized journey with a specific purpose.

Extinct No longer existing, as a species.

Habitat The natural home of a plant or animal.

Liberation Freedom from outside control.

Lichen A tiny fungus-like plant that grows on the surface of rocks and tree trunks.

Lynx A wild animal of the cat family, noted for its sharp eyesight.

Menagerie A collection of wild animals, kept for display.

Nocturnal animal An animal that is normally active at night and sleeps during the day.

Oryx A large straight-horned African antelope.

Poacher A person who hunts or fishes illegally.

Quarantine A period of time during which animals are kept apart to avoid passing infectious diseases to other animals.

Rain forest A thick tropical forest with heavy rainfall.

Reptile A cold-blooded animal that crawls or moves on its belly and usually has scaly skin.

Safari park An enclosed park in which wild animals are allowed to roam in the open and can be viewed by the public from their cars.

Species A group of animals that are alike in certain ways and can mate with one another to produce young.

Tarantulas A group of large, hairy spiders, some of which are poisonous.

Vaccinate To inject a substance made from the virus or germs that cause a disease, to give immunity against that disease.

Worm To free an animal from intestinal worms that cause disease.

Books to Read

All in the Family: Animal Species Around the World by Mary Elting. Putnam Publishing Group, 1984.

Animals Do the Strangest Things by Leonora Hornblow and Arthur Hornblow. Random House, 1965.

Animals Next Door: A Guide to Zoos and Aquariums of the Americas by Harry Gersh. Fleet Press, 1971.

The Answer Book About Animals by Mary Elting. Putnam Publishing Group, 1984.

What's New in the Zoo, Kangaroo? by Andra Tremper and Linda Diebort. Good Apple, 1982.

Zoos by Karen Jacobson. Children Press, 1982.

Zoos Without Cages by Judith E. Rinard. National Geographical Society, 1981.

Picture Acknowledgments

The photographs in this book were supplied by: Bruce Coleman 25; Frank Lane 6, 7, 8, 9, 10, 11, 12, 13, 14, 15, 16, 17, 18, 19, 20, 21, 22, 23, 26, 27, 28, 29; Mary Evans 5; Ronald Sheridan 4; Wayland 24. Cover picture by Zefa.

Index